for the
unheard, forgotten, perceptive

& unnecessarily sensitive.

written by pierre XO
illustrations by seffx

Black Mold -
(Stachybotrys chartarum)

-a type of toxic fungus that grows in hidden, poorly ventilated environments often due to neglect, abandonment & ignorance.

Toxic mold exposure

has also been linked to more serious, long-term effects:

memory loss,
insomnia,
anxiety,
depression,
trouble concentrating,
rage,
& confusion.

clouds are better
    cushion than iron.

        it'd be hard falling
            through these steps at least.

they say the grass is greener
                on the other side.

they must be right,
    there's barely any grass here.

                gotta make the most of it I guess.

if no one cares to
        water the yard,

                water it yourself.

should it
be so
hard to sit
in the sky?

bigger is better.
until it makes
you feel small.

A lot of self help books
will tell you;

"you are the source
        of your own suffering."

In that case,
    this dead-stop traffic
            is all my fault.

I wonder how Buddha
would feel being here.

I loved magic as a kid.

Turns out,
    I didn't need to look that hard
              to find an illusion.

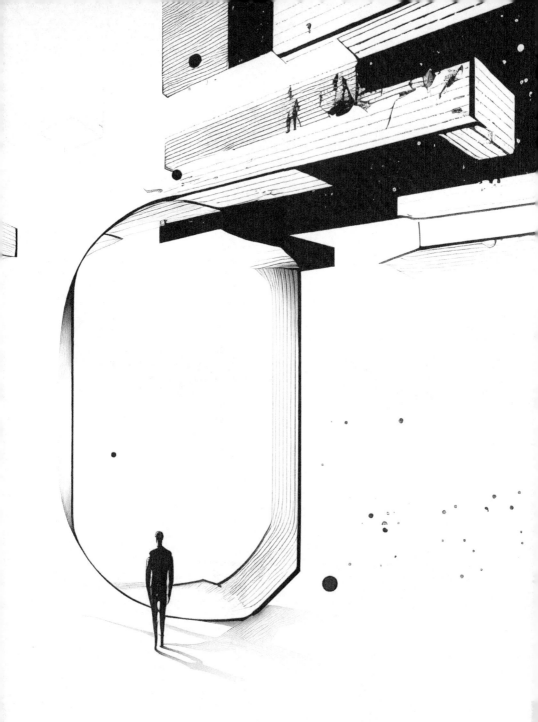

My soul itches & I can't reach it.

Emptiness isn't so bad sometimes.

A glass always full
loses its purpose eventually.

Wonder is universal.

I live for wonder.

Even space doesn't know
what it's expanding into.

I want to know more,
so I can continue
knowing less.

No matter who you might meet,

there's always something
　　　　you both don't know.

Strange how you and another
          can be in the same place,

                    & yet with completely
                          different backgrounds.

She'll walk around for hours
          as if she was looking for something.

                    I'll sit around for hours
                          not looking for anything.

We'll see all
the same places,
at different times.

We both might think
          that we're the only ones
                    feeling a certain way.

& this might be
          the reason why we are.

Everyone thinks the sun
    is a one-way ticket to happiness.

But really,
    it just makes the walk there
            unbearably hot.

I try hard not
to sink out here.

I try everything.

Maybe I'm just
not made
to be
on
a
boat.

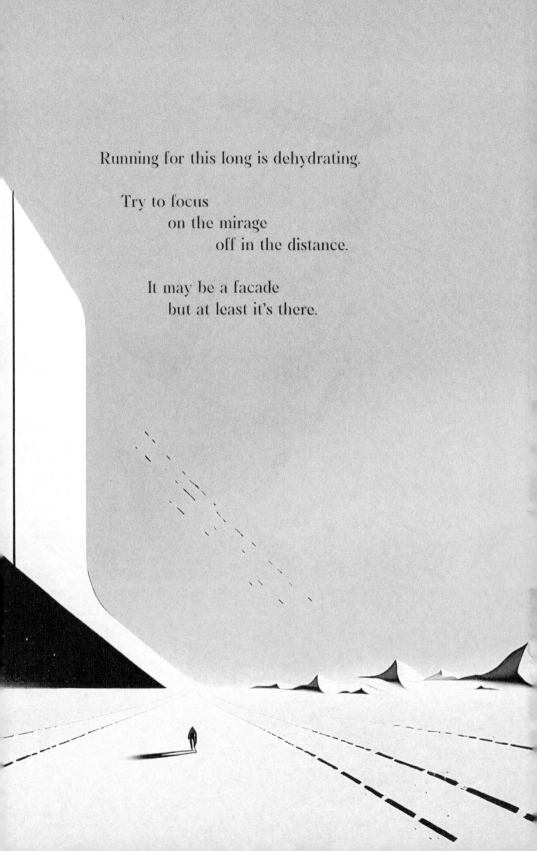

Running for this long is dehydrating.

Try to focus
        on the mirage
                off in the distance.

It may be a facade
        but at least it's there.

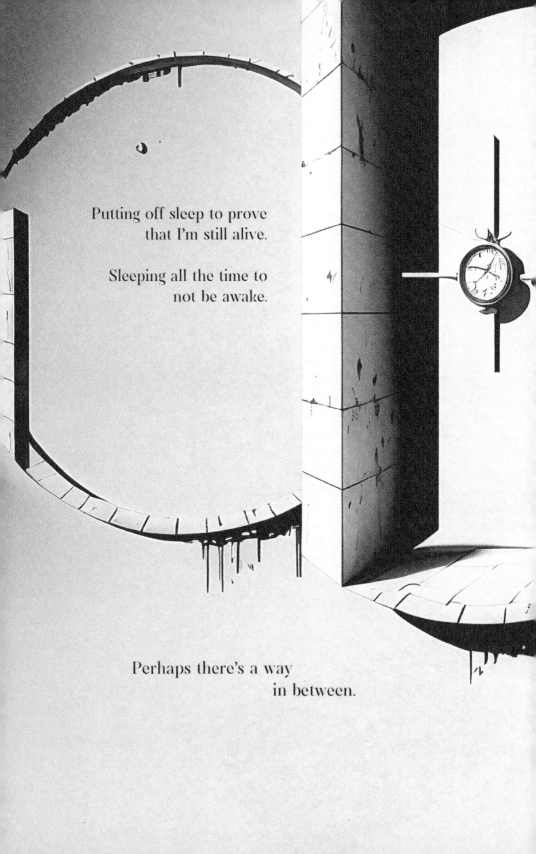

Putting off sleep to prove
that I'm still alive.

Sleeping all the time to
not be awake.

Perhaps there's a way
in between.

How many swipes
will it take
to leave me

emptier

than I started ?

All I want is to make an
impact on the world.

I hope there aren't
too many craters
already.

At least
the moon
is fine
with it.

Wow,
7:00 in
the morning.

The self-doubt should
come
    at any
        moment now.

Get up
    before it does.

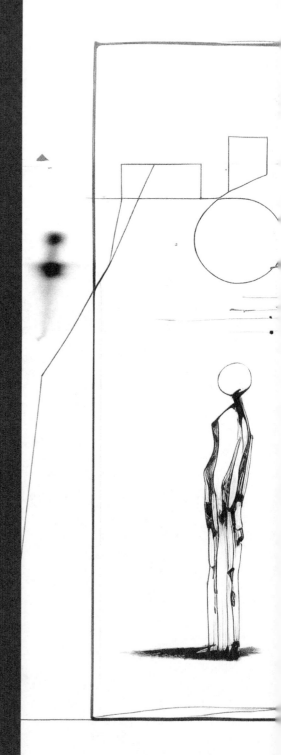

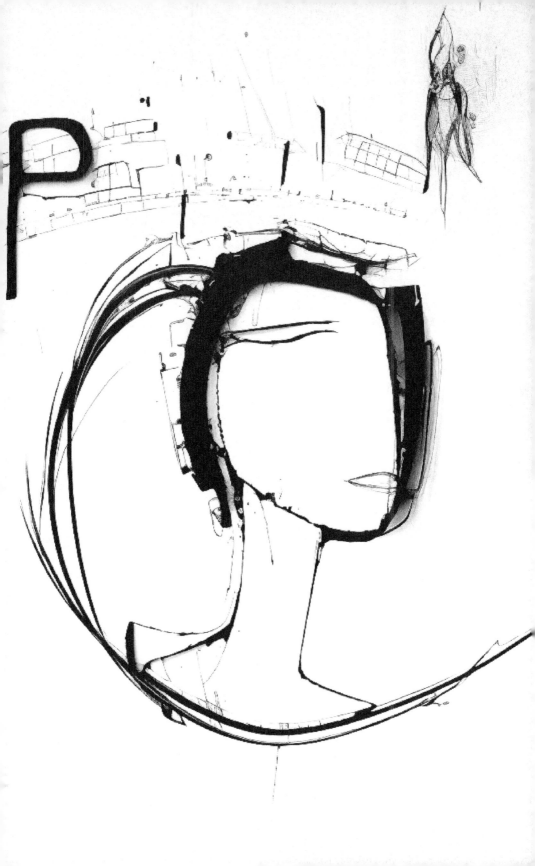

Cleanliness
    is next
       to Godliness.

I'm still waiting for him
         to show.

At least showering just feels good.

Who
needs friends,

when you
have
a
therapist?

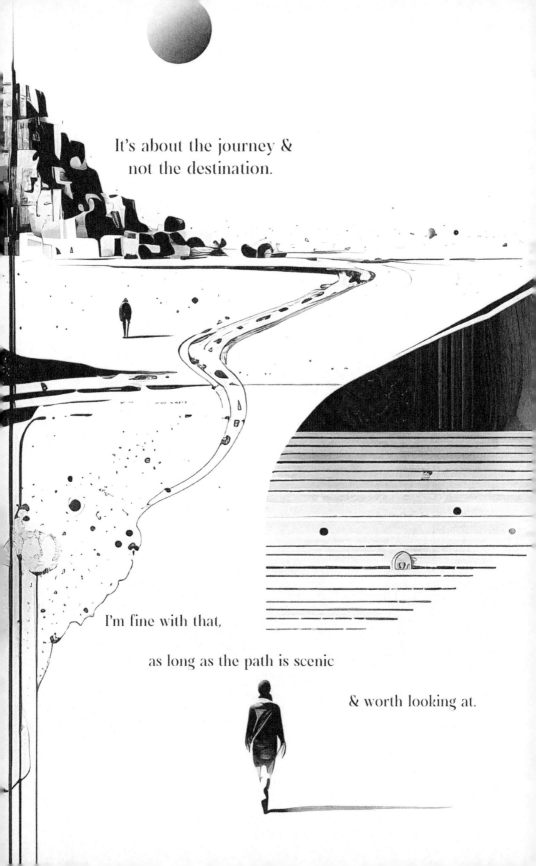

It's about the journey &
not the destination.

I'm fine with that,

as long as the path is scenic

& worth looking at.

"get off social media,"
because

disconnect

in real life
has more
flavor.

You do what
    they say everyday,

chipping away
    at your sculpture

            until you are nothing.

If you must
    chip at your sculpture,

chip the one
    you want to see.

social media is a
hug behind a
window

people forget,

in order
to bake a cake,

you have to
destroy the eggs.

I don't enjoy pain.

I'm lactose intolerant,

& everyone loves

ice cream.

a heart of gold
is worth nothing,

where the money
is paper.

it's a shame
that the most exciting
part of Jenga,

is when the tower falls.

what a pretty face.

I didn't say hi,

because I wanted it
          to stay pretty.

why better yourself
when you can complain?

all the time.
24/7
for the rest
of your life.

"You have a huge ego!"

They'll scream at you,

demanding that
        you listen

to their god-given
                authority.

if you lend a hand,

make sure theirs,

isn't heavier

than yours.

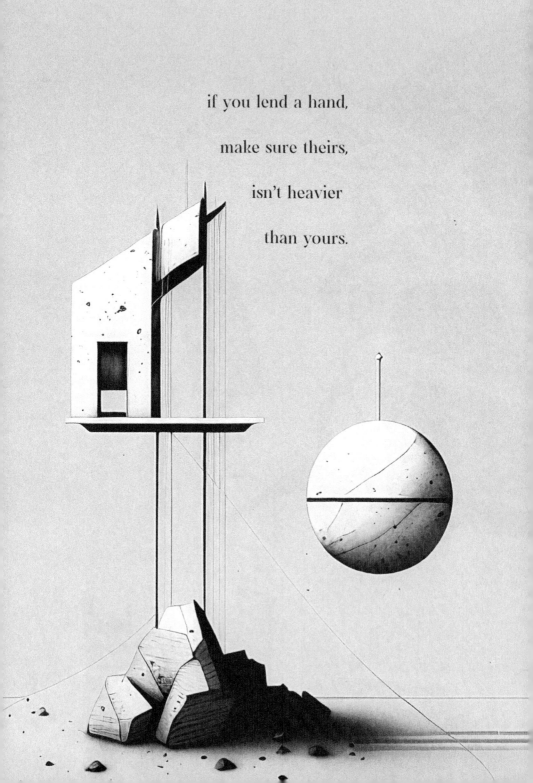

All I wanted
    was to dream,

& then the
        alarm went off.

Sometimes,
if I go back to sleep

I can continue it.

There are
      two sides to every story,

& I'm too busy
        writing my own,

while they're too busy to read It.

It'll take you.

It'll go where you
    need to go.

All you need to know
        is when to get on

            & when to get off.

Sometimes you just
    need to move.

Sometimes you'll end up
    where you started.

            Maybe,

    you'll get where
            you wanted to.

Most of the time,
    you'll end up where
            you needed to be.

In the end,
        you'll just

be glad you went.

A dreamer

in waking life

has insomnia.

A caged bird is fed.

It has a beautiful home.

Yet, all it wants to do.

is use its wings.

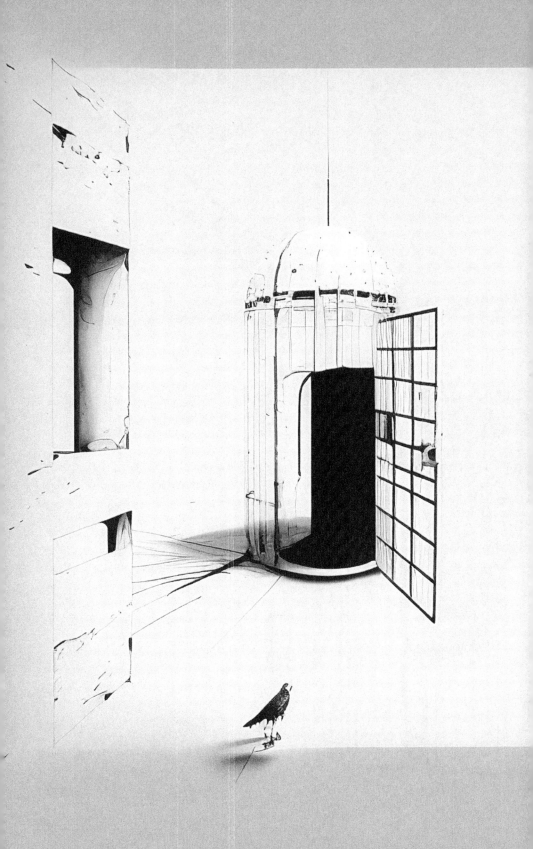

happiness
    is a firework,

lighting up the night sky.

it's harder to see
    in the daylight.

don't judge a book
by its cover.

too bad
no one reads.

love,
it would be easy.
if it were easy

to give to you.

love,
it would be easy,
if it were easy

to let it in.

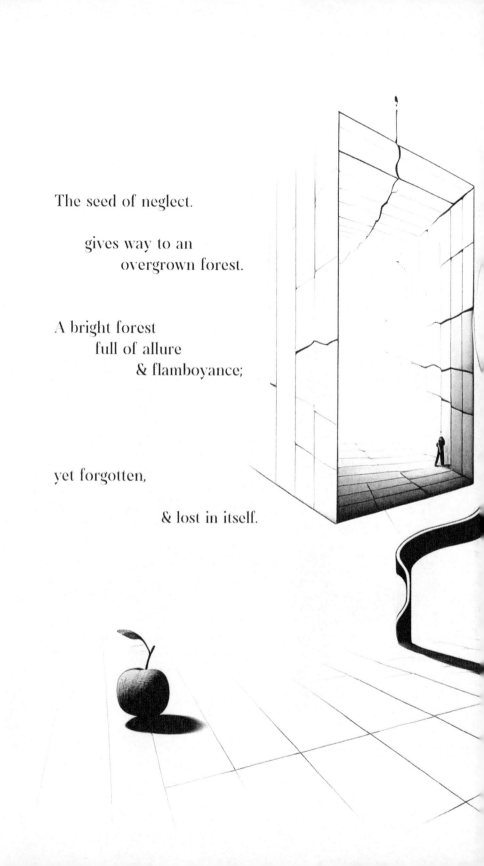

The seed of neglect.

gives way to an
overgrown forest.

A bright forest
full of allure
& flamboyance;

yet forgotten,

& lost in itself.

why must the reason

for the dawning of our birth,

be the cause of all the things we want

To break onto the shore?

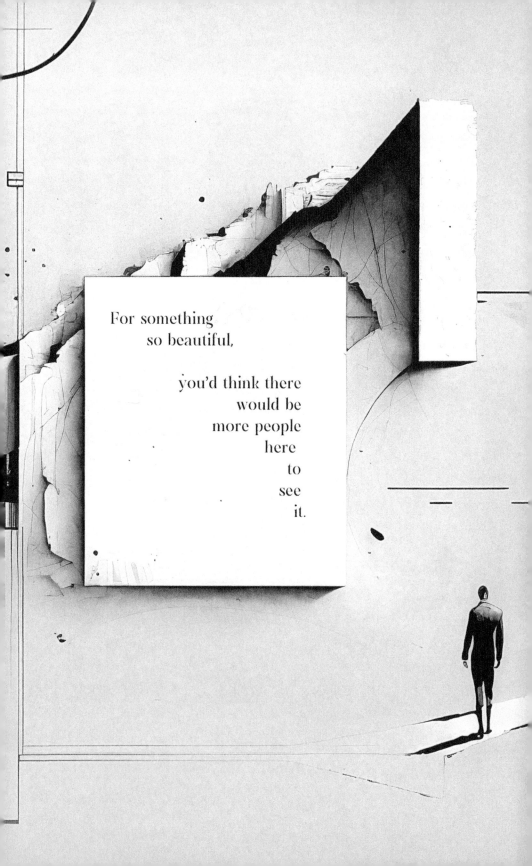

For something
   so beautiful,

      you'd think there
         would be
         more people
            here
               to
               see
                  it.

sometimes,

it takes the biggest outsider,

to know the inside.

Printed in Great Britain
by Amazon

20964461R00059